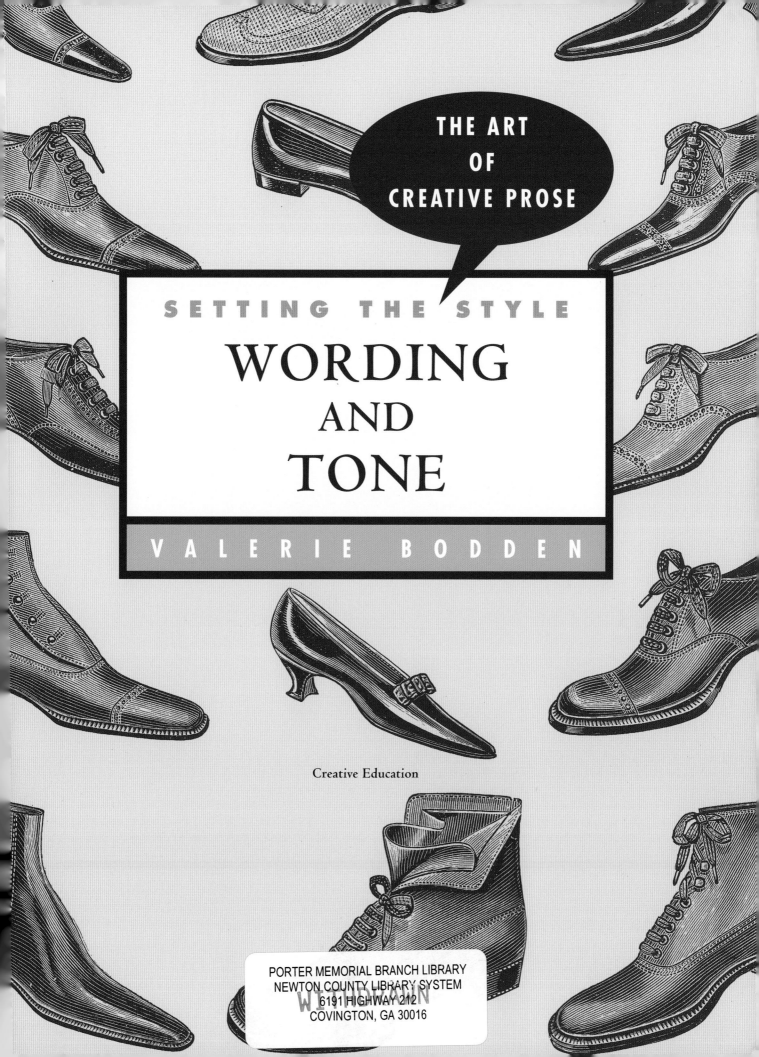

THE ART
OF
CREATIVE PROSE

SETTING THE STYLE

WORDING
AND
TONE

VALERIE BODDEN

Creative Education

Published by Creative Education
P.O. Box 227, Mankato, Minnesota 56002
Creative Education is an imprint of The Creative Company

Design by Stephanie Blumenthal
Production by The Design Lab
Art direction by Rita Marshall
Printed in the United States of America

Photographs by 123RF (Ken Pilon), Alamy (Mary Evans Picture Library), Corbis
(Bettmann, CORBIS SYGMA, Smithsonian Institution), Getty Images (Archive Photos,
Sara Countess of Essex, Loomis Dean//Time Life Pictures, Robert Frerck, Hulton Archive,
George Emil Libert, Carsten Peter), iStockphoto (Diana Didyk, Michael Flippo)

Excerpt on pages 16–17 by Ernest Hemingway, *A Farewell to Arms*.
New York: Simon & Schuster Inc., 1957, pp. 310–311

Library of Congress Cataloging-in-Publication Data

Bodden, Valerie.
Setting the style: wording and tone / by Valerie Bodden.
p. cm. — (The art of creative prose)
Includes index.
ISBN 978-1-58341-625-9
1. English language—Rhetoric. 2. English language—Style.
3. Creative writing. I. Title. II. Series.

PE1403.B63 2008
808'.042—dc22   2007019609

24689753

Introduction   5

The Literary in Literature   8

To the Point   14

The Sound on the Page   20

Setting the Tone   28

Breathing in the Atmosphere   34

Think Like a Writer   43

Glossary   46

Bibliography   47

Further Reading   47

Index   48

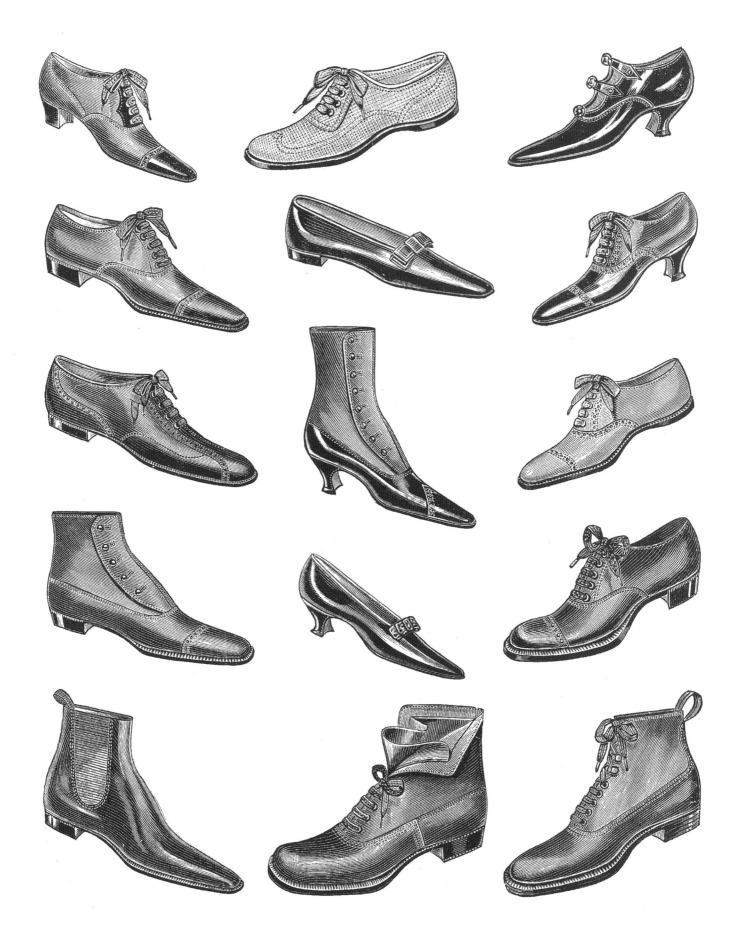

THE POWER OF CREATIVE PROSE IS AMAZING.

It can pull us into made-up lands and make us believe in things that never really happened. It can show us truths about our own life and lead us to see the world in a new way. It can make us laugh or cry—or do both at the same time. And all with words. Words, or more precisely, the way an author uses words—his style—can make a story a success or a failure. Style can also identify a story as coming from one author or another, for with his style an author marks his fiction as his own.

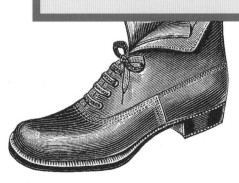

Style is the reason that thousands of books about war can be written—and no two of them end up alike. They may be about the same subject, but the styles of their authors—*how* each says what he says—set them apart. Even if you and a friend sat down to write the same book, with the same plot and characters, you would likely end up with two different stories. One of you might use short words and choppy sentences, with little **imagery**, while the other might write long, poetic sentences overflowing with **figurative** language. And that's a good thing. Having your own style means that you can write a story in a way that no one else could. As American author Katherine Anne Porter once put it, style is "the writer's own special way of telling a thing that makes it precisely his own and no one else's." It's your signature.

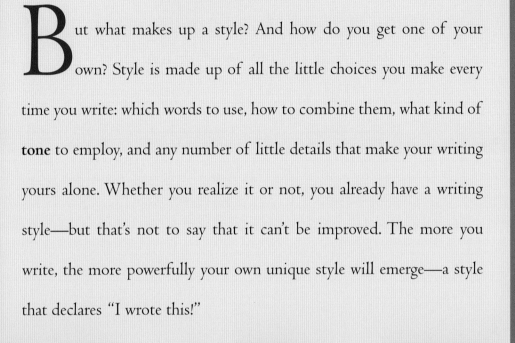

But what makes up a style? And how do you get one of your own? Style is made up of all the little choices you make every time you write: which words to use, how to combine them, what kind of **tone** to employ, and any number of little details that make your writing yours alone. Whether you realize it or not, you already have a writing style—but that's not to say that it can't be improved. The more you write, the more powerfully your own unique style will emerge—a style that declares "I wrote this!"

THE LITERARY

Just as there is an endless variety of writers, so too is there an endless variety of writing styles—one for every author who ever lived. Yet, in discussing style, it can be helpful to examine those styles that fall at opposite ends of the spectrum: "literary" or "artistic" style and "direct" or "journalistic" style. An artistic style is often poetic, placing as much emphasis on the words used as on what they mean. Such a style is often characterized by long, complex sentences made up of multi-syllabic words and elaborate imagery.

Although many beginning writers think that the only way to be a "real" author is to write in a literary manner, achieving this style without losing your story can be difficult. Even in a literary piece in which the focus is on style, the story and characters need to hold the reader's attention. In fact, if you write in a literary style, you may have to work extra hard to bring your story through in order to keep it from getting buried beneath the words. Otherwise, readers might become annoyed with trying to wade through your **prose** to figure out what is happening in your story. And they might get the feeling that you are trying too hard to impress them.

Used well, though, literary style can create beautiful images—and its words can create beautiful music. With a careful focus on imagery, figures of speech, and rhythm, such a style can help to color your story, making readers see—and feel—it in a different way than they would if the story were written in short, sparse prose. As you read the following excerpt from American author Nathaniel Hawthorne's novel *The Scarlet Letter* (1850), about a woman forced to wear a scarlet "A" on her clothing for her sin of adultery, pay close attention to the author's style, noting especially his word choice and sentence structure.

Nathaniel Hawthorne (1804–1864)

The door of the jail being flung open from within, there appeared, in the first place, like a black shadow emerging into sunshine, the grim and grisly presence of the town-beadle [minor church official], with a sword by his side, and his staff of office in his hand.... Stretching forth the official staff in his left hand, he laid his right upon the shoulder of a young woman, whom he thus drew forward; until, on the threshold of the prison-door, she repelled him, by an action marked with natural dignity and force of character, and stepped into the open air, as if by her own free will. She bore in her arms a child, a baby of some three months old, who winked and turned aside its little face from the too vivid light of day; because its existence, heretofore, had brought it acquainted only with the gray twilight of a dungeon, or other darksome apartment of the prison.

When the young woman—the mother of this child—stood fully revealed before the crowd, it seemed to be her first impulse to clasp the infant closely to her bosom; not so much by an impulse of motherly affection, as that she might thereby conceal a certain token, which was wrought or fastened into her dress. In a moment, however, wisely judging that one token of her shame would but poorly serve to hide another, she took the baby on her arm, and, with a burning blush, and yet a haughty smile, and a glance that would not be abashed, looked around at her townspeople and neighbors. On the breast of her gown, in fine red cloth, surrounded with an elaborate embroidery and fantastic flourishes of gold-thread, appeared the letter A. It was so artistically done, and with so much fertility and gorgeous luxuriance of fancy, that it had all the effect of a last and fitting decoration to the apparel which she wore; and which was of a splendor in accordance with the taste of the age, but greatly beyond what was allowed by the sumptuary [moral] regulations of the colony.

In just this short excerpt, we can get a clear feel for Hawthorne's style, which involves the use of long words and even longer sentences. Many of the words he uses—including "existence," "elaborate," "flourishes," "fertility," "luxuriance," and "apparel"—come from Latin roots, which makes them sound formal and flowing. Had Hawthorne chosen to use simpler, shorter words, he may have shown us a scarlet letter that was done not with "gorgeous luxuriance of fancy" but with "great creativity," and it may have decorated not the young woman's "apparel" but her "clothes." Such changes would give the text a much different feel.

Shorter sentences, too, would change Hawthorne's style. Imagine the first sentence of the excerpt rewritten in a more direct style: "The town-beadle flung open the door of the jail and stepped out. He had his sword by his side and his staff of office in his hand, and he seemed like a black shadow stepping into sunshine." Although these two shorter sentences say essentially the same thing as Hawthorne's longer sentence, they lose much of its artistry and flowing motion. The choppier style might fit another author's work, but not Hawthorne's.

Hawthorne doesn't use this formal, literary style in order to show off his large vocabulary or to impress readers with his ability to form complex sentences. Instead, his style serves to reflect the stiff, formal manners and morals of colonial America. If Hawthorne had written in a different style, he would have had a different story. Although the literary style isn't as common today as it was in Hawthorne's day, many modern authors do still use this technique to great effect. So sit down and try to think like Hawthorne. You may find it a struggle to write in a literary style—or you may find that the words flow easily from your pen, stretching into long, lyrical sentences that draw readers in with their beauty as much as their meaning.

TO THE POINT

Unlike authors who write in a literary style, in which the language of a story can become its focus, writers who employ a direct style try to tell a story without letting the words get in the way. This style, made famous by American author Ernest Hemingway in the 1930s and '40s and since utilized by countless writers, involves telling a story as simply and directly as possible. "Curt" stylists, as writers of this type of style are sometimes called, often use short words and sentences, with few adjectives (words that describe **nouns**), adverbs (words that describe **verbs**), or figures of speech.

Although a direct style may at first seem like an easy one in which to write, beginning authors shouldn't be fooled into thinking that this type of style involves no work. Figuring out how to present a **scene** in a direct, no-frills manner can be just as difficult as trying to come up with the perfect figure of speech to illustrate it. And, because a direct style relies so heavily on nouns and verbs, writers in this style must be careful to choose the right noun and the right verb for every sentence. In addition, it can be easy for curt stylists to slip into a **monotonous** sentence pattern. Just because a style is direct doesn't mean that it should become repetitious or boring.

O ne of the advantages of a direct style is that it can seem much more informal and conversational than a literary style, which makes it easier for most people to follow. As you read the following excerpt, taken from Hemingway's novel *A Farewell to Arms* (1929), about a World War I ambulance driver who leaves his duties, take note of how its style differs from that of *The Scarlet Letter*. Which do you think is easier to read?

Ernest Hemingway (1899–1961)

We stayed at that hotel three weeks. It was not bad; the dining-room was usually empty and very often we ate in our room at night. We walked in the town and took the cogwheel railway down to Ouchy and walked beside the lake. The weather became quite warm and it was like spring. We wished we were back in the mountains but the spring weather lasted only a few days and then the cold rawness of the breaking-up of winter came again.

Catherine bought the things she needed for the baby, up in the town. I went to a gymnasium in the arcade to box for exercise. I usually went up there in the morning while Catherine stayed late in bed. On the days of false spring it was very nice, after boxing and taking a shower, to walk along the streets smelling the spring in the air and stop at a café to sit and watch the people and read the paper and drink a vermouth [flavored wine]; then go down to the hotel and have lunch with Catherine. The professor at the boxing gymnasium wore mustaches and was very precise and jerky and went all to pieces if you started after him. But it was pleasant in the gym. There was good air and light and I worked quite hard, skipping rope, shadow boxing, doing abdominal exercises lying on the floor in a patch of sunlight that came through the open window, and occasionally scaring the professor when we boxed. I could not shadow-box in front of the narrow long mirror at first because it looked so strange to see a man with a beard boxing. But finally I just thought it was funny. I wanted to take off the beard as soon as I started boxing but Catherine did not want me to.

Sometimes Catherine and I went for rides out in the country in a carriage.... Catherine could not walk far now and I loved to ride out along the country roads with her. When there was a good day we had a splendid time and we never had a bad time.

As you read this excerpt, did you feel almost like you were reading a newspaper story or a journal entry? That's because Hemingway's direct style relies on simple words and a straightforward sentence structure. Rarely does he stray from the simple subject-verb-object sentence pattern (saying *who* did *what* to *whom*), which is the most basic sentence structure in the English language. At the same time, though, Hemingway varies his sentence length and pattern to maintain interest and avoid monotony. Thus, he often follows a short sentence with a longer sentence connected by a string of "ands" (such as "and stop at a café to sit and watch the people and read the paper and drink a vermouth"). In addition to adding interest to the rhythm of the prose, the use of so many **conjunctions** helps to carry the story forward and mimics real life, as we often do one thing and another and another at the same time.

In this excerpt, as in almost all of his writing, Hemingway stays as far away from adjectives and adverbs as possible. That is not to say that he doesn't offer vivid images, however. He just presents them simply, relying on the strength of the images rather than the beauty of the writing to make his point. Instead of crafting elaborate figures of speech to describe the weather, he simply states that the "cold rawness of the breaking-up of winter came again." Despite—or perhaps because of—its simplicity, this image gives us as clear a picture of the sharp cold of early spring as figurative language could. Hemingway's own writing philosophy was that "a writer's style should be direct and personal, his imagery rich and earthy, and his words simple and vigorous." Put his advice to the test and see what you come up with. Perhaps you'll find that your own style is close to Hemingway's. Or perhaps you'll find that—like most writers—your style falls somewhere between Hawthorne's and Hemingway's. Either way, you'll likely have new respect for the difficulties of writing simply.

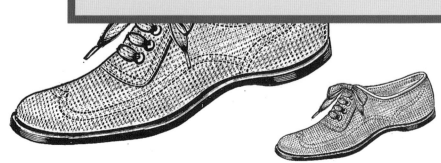

When you hear the term "rhythm," you probably think of music or poetry. But prose has rhythm, too. Although prose rhythm isn't created by rhyme or **meter** as is poetic rhythm, it is still created by the sound of the words on the page. Even when readers don't read a story aloud, they hear its words in their head. And if those words create a clumsy, awkward, or monotonous sound, readers will notice.

One of the best ways to improve your rhythm is to read your writing out loud. This will force you to listen to what readers will hear in their heads. As you read, think about the rhythm: Do your sentences vary in length and structure? Are there any sections that you stumble over? Do you use a variety of word lengths? Do any word combinations sound awkward?

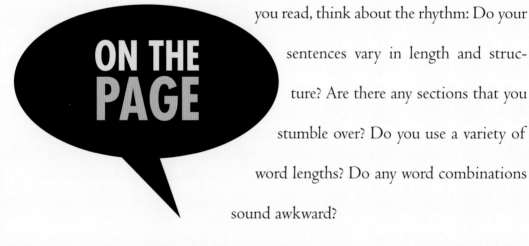

In about ten minutes time, Mr Fagin was seized with a fit of coughing, upon which Miss Nancy pulled her shawl over her shoulders, and declared it was time to go. Mr Sikes finding that he was reaching short apart

From a Manuscript of Dickens.
(Below, this passage from the note accompanying it :—" I should tell you perhaps as a kind of certificate of the Oliver scrap, that it is a portion of the original and only draught.   I never copy.")

P.S. I should tell you perhaps as a kind of certificate of the oliver scrap, that it is a portion of the original and only draught. — I never copy.

A written manuscript of Charles Dickens

As you examine your story's rhythm, you might also consider how rhythm affects meaning. A long, complex sentence made up of multi-syllabic words will slow the reader and might indicate slow, lazy movement, while a short sentence (or longer sentences broken up by commas or semi-colons) of one-syllable words can spur a reader's eye to the next sentence, indicating action and speed. Therefore, if you write all long, flowing sentences in a scene that should be action-packed, you might unintentionally slow the momentum of the scene.

Although prose rhythm comes largely from the sounds of words, it can also be found in the repetition of ideas, images, or **grammatical** constructions. For example, the technique of parallelism, in which two or more words or phrases follow the same pattern ("I came. I saw. I conquered."), creates a rhythm of its own. The related technique of antithesis, in which contrasting ideas are presented in parallel form, is another way of creating rhythm. In the opening paragraphs of his novel *A Tale of Two Cities* (1859), English author Charles Dickens uses both parallel construction and antithesis as he describes conditions in France and England before the start of the French Revolution.

Charles Dickens (1812–1870)

It was the best of times, it was the worst of times, it was the age of wisdom, it was the age of foolishness, it was the epoch of belief, it was the epoch of incredulity, it was the season of Light, it was the season of Darkness, it was the spring of hope, it was the winter of despair, we had everything before us, we had nothing before us, we were all going direct to Heaven, we were all going direct the other way—in short, the period was so far like the present period, that some of its noisiest authorities insisted on its being received, for good or for evil, in the superlative degree of comparison only.

There were a king with a large jaw, and a queen with a plain face, on the throne of England; there were a king with a large jaw, and a queen with a fair face, on the throne of France....

It was the year of Our Lord one thousand seven hundred and seventy-five. Spiritual revelations were conceded to England at that favoured period, as at this....

King Henrye the Seventh

France, less favoured on the whole as to matters spiritual than her sister of the shield and trident, rolled with exceeding smoothness down hill, making paper money and spending it. Under the guidance of her Christian pastors, she entertained herself, besides, with such humane achievements as sentencing a youth to have his hands cut off, his tongue torn out with pincers, and his body burned alive, because he had not kneeled down in the rain to do honour to a dirty procession of monks which passed within his view, at a distance of some fifty or sixty yards....

Environed by [these things],... those two of the large jaws, and those other two of the plain and the fair faces, trod with stir enough, and carried their divine rights with a high hand. Thus did the year one thousand seven hundred and seventy-five conduct their Greatnesses, and myriads of small creatures—the creatures of this chronicle among the rest—along the roads that lay before them.

With his sustained use of antithesis in the first sentence of the novel, Dickens draws readers in with his words and their musical structure. Read that sentence aloud. Do you find it easy to read, almost flowing off your tongue? Why do you think that is? Notice that in antithesis, every parallel phrase has the exact same structure. Dickens doesn't say, "It was the best of times, it was some of the worst times," but "It was the best of times, it was the worst of times." Changing the structure in any way from one phrase to the next would ruin the effect and rhythm of the sentence.

Elsewhere in the excerpt, Dickens uses parallelism to enhance rhythm. Some examples are obvious: in the first sentence of the second paragraph, Dickens describes the kings and queens of France and England in exactly the same words, with the exceptions of the adjectives "plain" and "fair" to characterize the queens' faces. Other instances of parallel construction are more subtle, such as "his hands cut off, his tongue torn out with pincers, and his body burned alive." In either case, the effect is the same, enhancing the overall rhythm and movement of the sentences.

The sound of Dickens's writing also contributes to its rhythm. By varying his word and sentence length, Dickens gives his prose a balanced feel. In addition, Dickens occasionally uses the technique of alliteration, in which two or more words with the same beginning sound are placed close together—for example, "present period," "fair face," "high hand," and "creatures of this chronicle." Used sparingly, this technique can help to create a musical sound and call attention to important words and ideas. So the next time you're thinking about rhythm, put away your drumsticks and take out your pen—then create some music on the page!

SETTING THE TONE

"Watch your tone, young man." "Don't take that tone with me, young lady." Have your parents ever said that to you? If they have, it's likely because they didn't like the attitude revealed by the **inflection** of your voice. You probably said something that would have sounded harmless enough if not for your sarcastic or sassy tone. And the reason you got a scolding is that tone can make a huge difference in meaning. For example, if your parents ask if you'd like to go out for pizza, you might respond, "I'd love to" with sincere enthusiasm. If, on the other hand, they ask if you'd like to take out the garbage, your response of "I'd love to" may be delivered in a sarcastic tone, meaning anything but that you'd love to do this chore.

Like people's voices, works of fiction also have tone. And tone in fiction means the same thing as it does in speech: attitude—or, more precisely, an author's attitude toward her subject. The tone of a story can be tragic, humorous, heroic, rough, despairing, sarcastic, or anything else the author feels. And almost everything on the page can help to reveal that tone—from word choice to pacing, description to **characterization**.

As a writer, you should think about the type of tone you'd like your story to have before you begin to write. In thinking about tone, bear in mind that any story can have any type of tone. A war story doesn't have to be tragic, and a romance doesn't have to be lighthearted. At the same time, you will usually want to keep your tone consistent throughout a story. That's not to say that a comedy can't have sad scenes, but those scenes probably shouldn't shift too far from the story's humorous tone. Otherwise, readers might be jolted by the inconsistency and left puzzled about how they should feel.

In some stories, tone is quite subtle, while in others it may be easy to identify. Spanish author Miguel de Cervantes establishes a rather obvious tone in the following excerpt from his classic novel *The History of Don Quixote de la Mancha* (1605), about a man who reads so much about knights that he decides to become one—even taking on a squire named Sancho Panza—despite the fact that the age of knighthood has long since come to an end. How would you define the tone of this piece?

At this point [Don Quixote and Sancho Panza] came in sight of thirty or forty wind-mills that there are on that plain, and as soon as Don Quixote saw them he said to his squire, "Fortune is arranging matters for us better than we could have shaped our desires ourselves, for look there, friend Sancho Panza, where thirty or more monstrous giants present themselves, all of whom I mean to engage in battle and slay, and with whose spoils we shall begin to make our fortunes...."

"What giants?" said Sancho Panza.

"Those thou seest there," answered his master, "with the long arms, and some have them nearly two leagues long."

"Look, your worship," said Sancho; "what we see there are not giants but windmills...."

"It is easy to see," replied Don Quixote, "that thou art not used to this business of adventures; those are giants; and if thou art afraid, away with thee...and betake thyself to prayer while I engage them in fierce and unequal combat."

So saying, he gave the spur to his steed Rocinante, heedless of the cries his squire Sancho sent after him, warning him that most certainly they were windmills and not giants he was going to attack. He, however, was so positive they were giants that he neither heard the cries of Sancho, nor perceived, near as he was, what they were, but made at them shouting, "Fly not, cowards and vile beings, for it is a single knight that attacks you."

A slight breeze at this moment sprang up, and the great sails began to move, seeing which Don Quixote exclaimed, "Though ye flourish more arms than the giant Briareus, ye have to reckon with me."

So saying,...he charged at Rocinante's fullest gallop and fell upon the first mill that stood in front of him; but as he drove his lance-point into the sail the wind whirled it round with such force that it shivered the lance to pieces, sweeping with it horse and rider, who went rolling over on the plain, in a sorry condition.

Miguel de Cervantes (1547–1616)

As you read this excerpt, did you find yourself chuckling? That's because Cervantes has adopted a comic tone in this work, which mocks the romantic books of chivalry popular in his day. In order to establish his humorous tone, Cervantes first gives us a comic character in Don Quixote, who sees the world not as it really is, but as he wants to see it. Because of this, Cervantes is able to set up improbable scenes, in which a man takes up arms against a windmill, proclaiming that it is a giant that he must vanquish.

The humor of the scene lies not only in Don Quixote's foolish actions, but also in the contrast between him and Sancho Panza. The supposedly subservient squire is obviously more sensible than his master, and his language in warning Quixote that he is attacking windmills, not giants, is straightforward, in contrast to Quixote's over-romanticized "knightly" speech. Although this excerpt ends with both Don Quixote and his horse injured, we are unlikely to feel too badly for the knight, for even here Cervantes doesn't stray from his comic tone to tell us of Quixote's serious injuries. Instead, he says that he was "in a sorry condition"—probably an understatement after doing battle with a windmill! With careful attention to tone, you too can create fiction that has readers laughing out loud—or sobbing into their books. So the next time you begin to write, ignore your parents' warnings about tone and infuse your work with attitude, whatever that attitude may be!

Have you ever picked up a book and been scared to turn the page, not necessarily because of what was happening, but because of how it felt? Maybe its "atmosphere" was creepy or oppressive or ominous. In fiction, atmosphere—or how the story feels—is created by a combination of the author's tone and his descriptions of the setting. For example, a spooky atmosphere might be created by an author's description of a dark forest and haunting sounds, combined with a tone of fear or trepidation. A completely different atmosphere would be created if the author described the same setting in a comic or defiant tone, while yet another atmosphere would be evoked if the author described a daylight setting in a fearful tone.

As you write, you should consider whether or not your atmosphere is creating the right mood in your readers. Do you want them to be scared? Then you'll want to make sure that your descriptions and tone convey a scary atmosphere. Do you want them to feel like children at the circus? Then you'll need descriptions and a tone that reflect the lighthearted atmosphere of the circus. In order to establish the right atmosphere for your story, think about the time of day (daytime evokes a different atmosphere than nighttime), the weather (rain creates a different mood than sunshine), and sensory impressions (dampness feels different than heat). Simply telling your readers what the atmosphere was like—for example, "It was a dark and scary night"—is unlikely to stir up strong emotions in them. Making them feel that atmosphere for themselves, on the other hand, can draw them into the story and make them feel the same terror or tranquility as your characters feel.

As you read the following excerpt from Irish author Bram Stoker's novel *Dracula* (1897), notice how its description and tone help to create an ominous, threatening atmosphere as the narrator, Jonathan Harker, tells about his carriage trip through Transylvania to Count Dracula's home.

By-and-by, however, as I was curious to know how time was passing, I struck a match, and by its flame looked at my watch; it was within a few minutes of midnight. This gave me a sort of shock, for I suppose the general superstition about midnight was increased by my recent experiences. I waited with a sick feeling of suspense.

Then a dog began to howl somewhere in a farmhouse far down the road—a long agonized wailing, as if from fear. The sound was taken up by another dog, and then another and another, till, borne on the wind which now sighed softly through the Pass, a wild howling began, which seemed to come from all over the country, as far as the imagination could grasp it through the gloom of the night. At the first howl the horses began to strain and rear, but the driver spoke to them soothingly, and they quieted down.... Then, far off in the distance, from the mountains on each side of us began a louder and a sharper howling—that of wolves—which affected both the horses and myself in the same way—for I was minded to jump from the calèche [carriage] and run, whilst they reared again and plunged madly....

Soon we were hemmed in with trees, which in places arched right over the roadway till we passed as through a tunnel; and again great frowning rocks guarded us boldly on either side. Though we were in shelter, we could hear the rising wind, for it moaned and whistled through the rocks, and the branches of the trees crashed together as we swept along. It grew colder and colder still, and fine, powdery snow began to fall, so that soon we and all around us were covered with a white blanket. The keen wind still carried the howling of the dogs, though this grew fainter as we went on our way. The baying of the wolves sounded nearer and nearer, as though they were closing round on us from every side.

At this point in the story, Jonathan Harker does not yet know that Count Dracula is a vampire—or even that it is the count himself who is driving the carriage. Yet, he is afraid—afraid not of the count, but of the atmosphere of Transylvania. As we read this excerpt, we can almost feel the hairs on the back of Jonathan's neck stand up in the cold, midnight air as his ears pick up the eerie howling of the dogs and wolves. And *we* start to feel nervous too. Besides simply telling us that Jonathan felt scared and "sick" with suspense, Stoker uses carefully chosen descriptions to convey the forbidding atmosphere directly to us. With words such as "hemmed in" and "guarded," we start to feel trapped in this ominous environment, and the moaning wind and "crashing" trees add to our sense of unease. Even the snowfall, which, if described in another way and another setting may have seemed peaceful, adds to our feeling of dread.

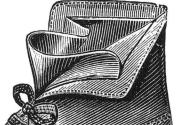

With his straightforward, solemn tone, Stoker helps us to sense the seriousness of the situation. We aren't tempted to think that Harker is imagining or exaggerating the creepiness of his surroundings or that his adventure is like a Halloween hayride—scary for a time, but really just for fun. Instead, we realize that Harker is in real danger in this country. Had Stoker used a comic tone or a calm, sunlit setting, he would not have been able to establish the same atmosphere—and thus would have been unable to write the same book.

With so many possibilities for atmosphere, tone, and style, it's no wonder there are so many different stories out there—and so many more waiting to be written. The English language allows for an infinite number of ways to combine words and express ideas—but only one way is yours alone. So sit down and put your pen to the paper. Soon, your words will begin to speak for themselves, stamping your signature on everything you write!

Bram Stoker (1847–1912)

Despite the fact that style is something that

THINK LIKE A WRITER

is uniquely yours, it won't come to you overnight.

Since the only way to hone your style is to read various styles and

to practice writing in your own, use the following exercises to help you get

started thinking about style and tone.

LITERARY LITERATURE Many authors in the 18th and 19th centuries wrote

in a literary style, with long sentences and formal word choices. Find a work

by a prominent 18th- or 19th-century author (such as Jane Austen or Samuel

Johnson) and read it with a careful eye (and ear) for style. After you've finished,

think about a more **contemporary** piece that you've read recently. Which did

you like better? Does the reason have anything to do with the author's style?

Do you think the older work could have been written in another style? Would

it have had the same effect?

TRYING ON NEW STYLES Find stories from three authors who write in dif-

ferent styles (for example, Ernest Hemingway, John Steinbeck, and J. K. Rowling).

Read a page or two from each work, taking careful note of the style. Now, try to

write a short scene (about a trip, for example) in each author's style. The details of the scene should remain the same from one piece to the next; only the style will differ. When you're done, think about which style seemed the most natural to write in. Which was the most difficult? As you develop your own style, you won't want to copy another author's style exactly—but practicing doing so can help you identify the stylistic tendencies that feel right for you.

THE POETRY OF PROSE In order to become more aware of the rhythm in prose, it can be helpful to read poetry, which forces you to pay careful attention to the sound of each line. Before you begin writing your next prose piece, sit down and read a poem by any author. Now, try to convert that poem into prose, continuing to pay attention to the sound of each line. When you're done, read your prose out loud into a tape recorder. Then play back your recording, listening for any awkward or clumsy spots or places where the rhythm becomes monotonous because of unvarying word or sentence lengths. Fix any problem areas and reread your piece until you are satisfied that it sings with the right rhythm.

CHANGING YOUR TONE In order to begin to recognize how a change in tone can result in a change in meaning, write a scene that begins with the line "She knew it couldn't last forever" using a tragic tone. When you're done, rewrite the same scene—beginning with the same line—in a comic tone. Then come up with two other tones in which to write the scene (for example, sarcastic, mocking, or romantic). As you write, remember that word choice, characterization, and dialogue can all have a strong effect on tone. When you're done, decide which scene works best and develop it into a short story, being careful to keep your tone consistent throughout.

ATMOSPHERIC CONDITIONS Think about a time when you were scared of something. Maybe it was in the middle of a terrible storm. Maybe you were by yourself at night. Maybe you knew you were about to be yelled at. Now think about all of the factors that combined to make you scared. Were there ominous storm clouds? Was a branch tapping on your bedroom window? Did you see your mom's angry expression? Try to recreate the atmosphere of your experience in writing, conveying by both your description and your tone the feel of the scene. When you're done, reread what you've written. If the atmosphere isn't strong enough, go back and add some more details—either real or made-up—until readers will be scared for you as they read your piece.

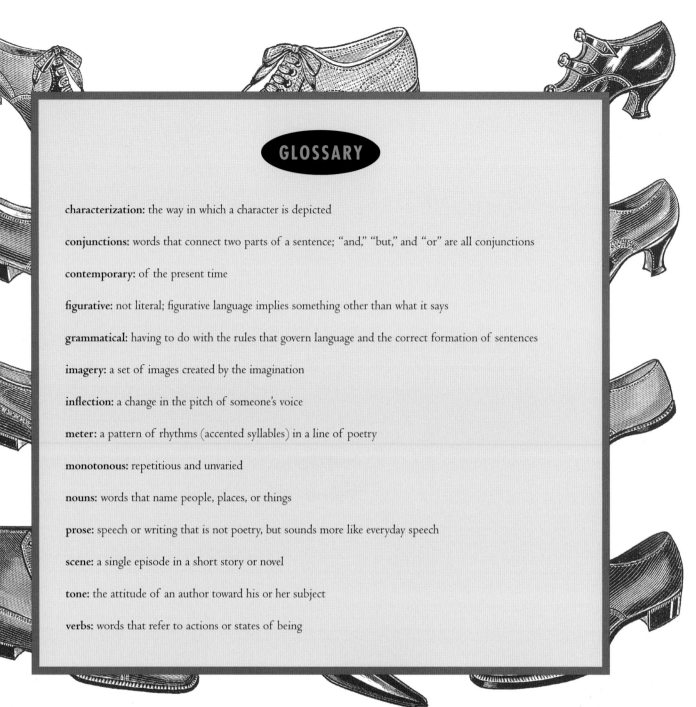

GLOSSARY

characterization: the way in which a character is depicted

conjunctions: words that connect two parts of a sentence; "and," "but," and "or" are all conjunctions

contemporary: of the present time

figurative: not literal; figurative language implies something other than what it says

grammatical: having to do with the rules that govern language and the correct formation of sentences

imagery: a set of images created by the imagination

inflection: a change in the pitch of someone's voice

meter: a pattern of rhythms (accented syllables) in a line of poetry

monotonous: repetitious and unvaried

nouns: words that name people, places, or things

prose: speech or writing that is not poetry, but sounds more like everyday speech

scene: a single episode in a short story or novel

tone: the attitude of an author toward his or her subject

verbs: words that refer to actions or states of being

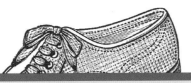

BIBLIOGRAPHY

Burroway, Janet. *Writing Fiction: A Guide to Narrative Craft*. New York: HarperCollins, 1987.

Clark, Matthew. *A Matter of Style*. Ontario: Oxford University Press, 2002.

Conrad, Barnaby. *The Complete Guide to Writing Fiction*. Cincinnati, Ohio: Writer's Digest Books, 1990.

Glaser, Joe. *Understanding Style: Practical Ways to Improve Your Writing*. New York: Oxford University Press, 1999.

Macauley, Robie, and George Lanning. *Technique in Fiction*. New York: St. Martin's Press, 1987.

Rubie, Peter. *The Elements of Storytelling*. New York: John Wiley & Sons, 1996.

Wilcox, Earl, and David Rankin. *Fundamentals of Fiction*. New York: University Press of America, 1993.

Yagoda, Ben. *The Sound on the Page: Style and Voice in Writing*. New York: HarperResource, 2004.

FURTHER READING

Cervantes, Miguel de. *The History of Don Quixote de la Mancha*. Translated by John Ormsby. Chicago: Encyclopædia Britannica, 1952.

Dickens, Charles. *A Tale of Two Cities*. New York: Signet Classic, 1997.

Hawthorne, Nathaniel. *The Scarlet Letter*. New York: Bantam Books, 1986.

Hemingway, Ernest. *A Farewell to Arms*. New York: Scribner Paperback Fiction, 1995.

Stoker, Bram. *Dracula*. New York: Barnes & Noble Classics, 2003.

INDEX

alliteration 27

antithesis 22, 26

atmosphere 34–35, 40–41, 45

Cervantes, Miguel de 29–31, 33

   The History of Don Quixote de la Mancha 29–31, 33

description 34, 35, 40, 45

Dickens, Charles 22, 24–27

   A Tale of Two Cities 22, 24–27

Hawthorne, Nathaniel 9–10, 12–13, 19

   The Scarlet Letter 9–10, 12–13, 15

Hemingway, Ernest 14, 15–19, 43

   A Farewell to Arms 15–19

parallelism 22, 26

poetry 20, 44

prose rhythm 18, 20, 22, 26–27, 44

sentence length 6, 8, 9, 12, 13, 14, 18, 20, 22, 27, 44

sentence patterns 14, 18, 20, 22, 26, 27

Stoker, Bram 35, 37–38, 40–41

   Dracula 35, 37–38, 40–41

tone 7, 28–29, 33, 34, 35, 41, 44–45

word choice 5, 7, 8, 12, 14, 18, 19, 20, 22, 27, 28, 40, 45

writing styles

   direct 8, 9, 12, 14–15, 18–19

   literary 8–9, 12–13, 14, 15, 43